Inside My Body

How do my muscles get strong?

Steve Parker

www.raintreepublishers.co.uk
Visit our website to find out
more information about
Raintree books.

To order:
☎ Phone 0845 6044371
🖹 Fax +44 (0) 1865 312263
✉ Email myorders@raintreepublishers.co.uk

Customers from outside the UK please telephone +44 1865 312262

Raintree is an imprint of Capstone Global Library Limited,
a company incorporated in England and Wales having its
registered office at 7 Pilgrim Street, London, EC4V 6LB –
Registered company number: 6695582

Text © Capstone Global Library Limited 2011
First published in hardback in 2011
Paperback edition first published in 2012
The moral rights of the proprietor have been asserted.

Edited by Kate de Villiers and Laura Knowles
Designed by Steve Mead
Illustrations by KJA-Artists.com
Picture research by Mica Brancic
Originated by Capstone Global Library Ltd
Printed and bound in China by CTPS

ISBN 978 1 406 22106 0 (hardback)
14 13 12 11 10
10 9 8 7 6 5 4 3 2 1

ISBN 978 1 406 22118 3 (paperback)
15 14 13 12 11
10 9 8 7 6 5 4 3 2 1

British Library Cataloguing in Publication Data
Parker, Steve
How do my muscles get strong?. -- (Inside my body)
612.7'4-dc22
A full catalogue record for this book is available from the
British Library.

Acknowledgements
We would like to thank the following for permission to
reproduce photographs: Corbis p. **17** (© Randy Faris);
Getty Images p. **25** (AFP/Patrik Stollarz); NASA p. **13**;
Photolibrary pp. **4** (Corbis), **8** (Phototake Science/Eric
Grave), **11** (Photoalto/Odilon Dimier), **12** (imagebroker.
net/Uwe Umstätter), **15** (Somos Images), **16** (Moodboard
RF), **19** (AFLO Royalty Free/Koji Aoki), **18** (Polka Dot
Images/Jupiterimages Jupiterimages), **20** (Imagestate RM/
Adrian Peacock), **23** (Medicimage), **27** (Image Source).

Photographic design details reproduced with permission
of Science Photo Library p. **6** (Gustoimages); Shutterstock
pp. **15**, **18**, **25** (© Isaac Marzioli), **15**, **18**, **25** (© Yurok).

Cover photograph of boys flexing muscles reproduced
with permission of Getty Images/Workbook Stock/
Jupiterimages.

We would like to thank David Wright for his invaluable
help in the preparation of this book.

Every effort has been made to contact copyright holders
of any material reproduced in this book. Any omissions
will be rectified in subsequent printings if notice is given
to the publisher.

Contents

Words that appear in the text in bold, **like this**, are explained in the glossary on page 30.

How strong can I get?

Most people can become very strong! Strength depends on muscles. Everyone has the same number of muscles. Everyone can make their muscles bigger and stronger by using them regularly, keeping active, and doing exercise.

🔍 **Pull harder! A tug of war is a tiring test of your muscles' pulling power.**

What do muscles do?

Muscles make you move. Without them, you could not walk, eat, write, or even blink. Every action you make is muscle-powered. Without the muscles in your chest, you could not breathe. Even your heart, which pumps blood around your body, is a muscle.

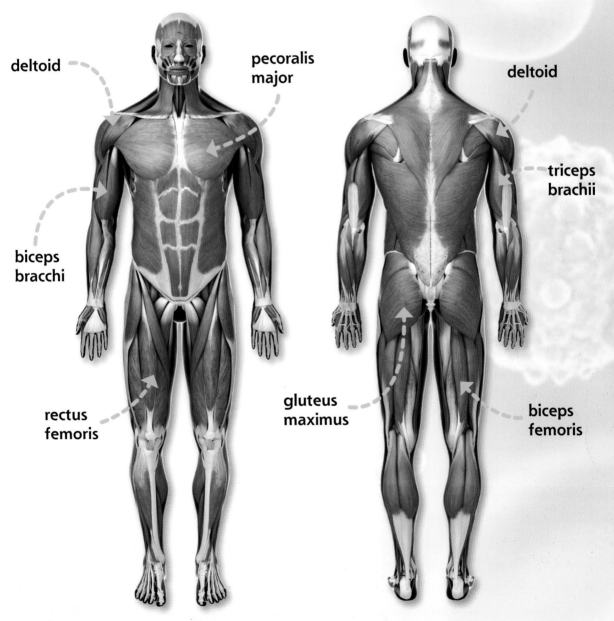

deltoid

pecoralis major

deltoid

triceps brachii

biceps bracchi

rectus femoris

gluteus maximus

biceps femoris

This is what your muscles look like under your skin. Some of the main muscles have been labelled with their scientific names.

How many muscles do I have?

The human body has more muscles than most people think – over 640! Some are big and powerful, especially those in your back and legs. Other muscles are tiny and delicate.

Movement muscles

Your body has about 300 muscles that attach to the skeleton. These are called **skeletal muscles**. Each muscle is joined to a bone at each end. As the muscle pulls, it moves the bones and that part of your body. Skeletal muscles are also known as voluntary muscles, because you can control how they move.

🔍 **A CT scan "sees" inside the body. In this view, the large blue areas are muscles in the hips and upper thighs. The two big, greenish-yellow parts are the thigh bones.**

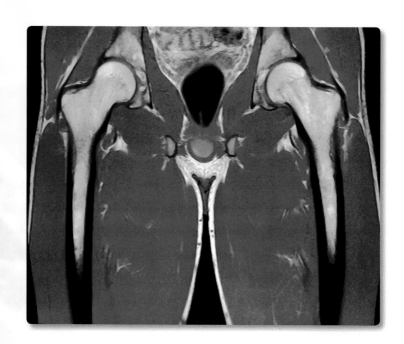

Other kinds of muscles

Your body also has about 300 more muscles inside organs. These are called **smooth muscles**. There is also one very special muscle, which the heart is made from. This is called **cardiac muscle**. These muscles are involuntary muscles, which means they work without you thinking about it.

Muscle names

Every muscle has its own scientific name. Often this describes its size and shape, and perhaps where it is in the body. Some muscles also have everyday names. The table below shows some of these muscles, and what their names mean.

Everyday name	Scientific name	Where are they?	Meaning
Pecs	Pectoralis major	Upper chest near each shoulder	*Pectoralis* means "to do with the shoulder". *Major* means "big (muscle)".
Delts	Deltoid	One over each shoulder	"Shaped like a triangle"
Glutes	Gluteus maximus	One in each buttock	*Gluteus* means "to do with the buttocks". *Maximus* means "biggest (muscle of its type)".

What is inside a muscle?

Muscles are many different sizes and shapes, but inside they all look very similar. The main parts inside are bundles of **muscle fibres**, which are thinner than hairs.

SCIENCE BEHIND THE MYTH

MYTH: If you don't use your muscles they disappear.

SCIENCE: If muscles are not used much, they become smaller and weaker. But they never disappear. If you start to use them again, they soon get bigger and stronger.

Look at **skeletal muscle** under a microscope and you see a stripy or banding pattern. That's why this type of muscle is also known as striped or striated muscle.

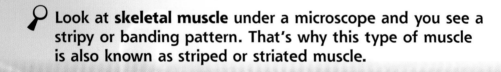

Fibres and fibrils

Bigger muscles have more fibres than smaller muscles. As you exercise your muscles, they get bigger by growing more fibres.

Inside muscle fibres are bundles of even smaller string-like parts called **myofibrils**. These fibrils contain long **protein filaments**. It is these protein filaments that can make a muscle **contract** (get shorter) by sliding past each other. Inside a muscle there are also **blood vessels**. These bring high-energy substances for the muscle to use as it works.

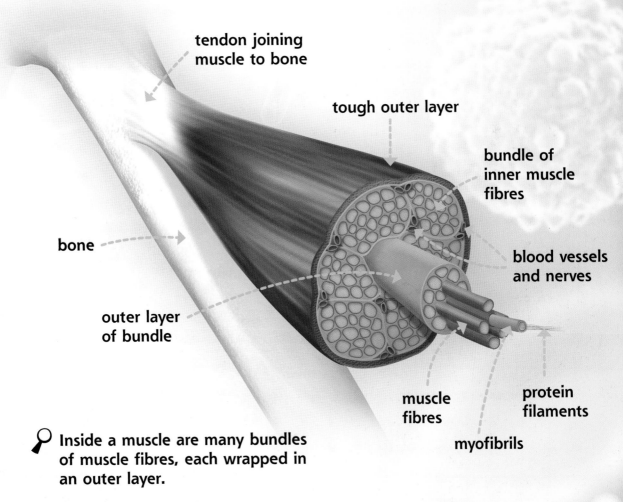

tendon joining muscle to bone

tough outer layer

bundle of inner muscle fibres

bone

blood vessels and nerves

outer layer of bundle

muscle fibres

protein filaments

myofibrils

Inside a muscle are many bundles of muscle fibres, each wrapped in an outer layer.

How do muscles work?

Muscles work in a very simple way. They **contract** (get shorter). As **skeletal muscles** contract, they pull on the bones. Strong, rope-like parts called **tendons**, join muscles to their bones.

Pull not push

Try bending your elbow. The biceps brachii muscle in your upper arm contracts and pulls your lower arm bone. You can see and feel the biceps bulge as it contracts. But the biceps cannot push to straighten your elbow, because muscles can only pull. So another muscle on the underside of your upper arm, the triceps brachii, pulls to straighten your elbow.

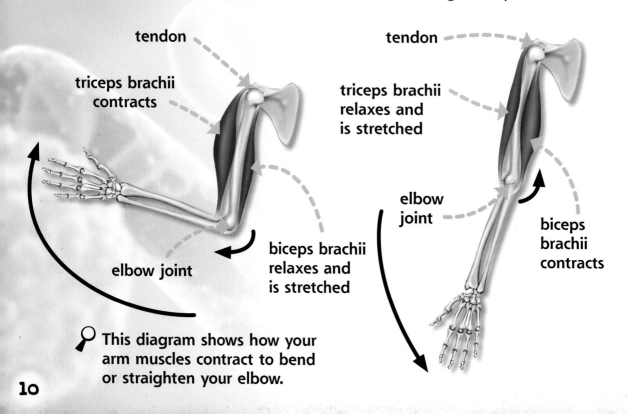

tendon

triceps brachii contracts

elbow joint

biceps brachii relaxes and is stretched

tendon

triceps brachii relaxes and is stretched

elbow joint

biceps brachii contracts

🔍 This diagram shows how your arm muscles contract to bend or straighten your elbow.

Teamwork

All over your body, one muscle pulls a body part one way, and then another muscle pulls it back. In fact, for most movements there are not just two muscles but 10, 20, or more. They work as a team for smooth, steady movements.

Working out with weights makes the shoulder deltoid muscles and the biceps brachii muscles bulge.

How do I keep my muscles healthy?

To stay healthy, muscles must be active. They need to make movements and do exercises. Lazy muscles become weaker and less healthy.

🔍 **Having fun with friends, cycling and skateboarding, is a great way to be active.**

Action all day

Sport and exercise are very good for muscles. Apart from organized sport and exercise, there are many ways to keep your muscles active in daily life. For example:

- Cycle somewhere (if it's safe) rather than go in the car.
- Use the stairs instead of a lift.
- Keep on the move while out with friends, rather than sitting around.
- Help with chores at home, rather than sitting in front of the computer or television.

Many benefits of exercise

Sport and exercise help your **skeletal muscles** and they also have many healthy effects on the rest of your body.

- Your heart stays strong and beats powerfully.
- Your breathing muscles work well so your lungs take in enough air.
- Your joints stay flexible and bend easily.
- Busy muscles use energy from your food. If this energy was not used, the body would store it as fat.

SCIENCE BEHIND THE MYTH

MYTH: Astronauts take it easy in space

SCIENCE: Not true! Astronauts have lots of scientific work to do. They also take plenty of exercise, using equipment such as exercise bikes. This is because there is no pulling force of gravity for their muscles to work against. Without exercise, their muscles would soon become weak and floppy.

What is good exercise?

Almost any kind of exercise or activity is good for your muscles and your body. But certain kinds of exercise and sport are better than others because they involve many muscles around the body.

Regular and often

- Regular exercise or sport, three or four times each week, is much better than a long session once every few weeks.
- To have the best effect, exercise should last at least 20–30 minutes.
- The exercise or activity should be hard enough to make you breathe faster and speed up your **pulse rate**. This shows that the exercise is helping your heart, lungs, and your whole body.

SCIENCE BEHIND THE MYTH

MYTH: Exercise is a waste of energy.

SCIENCE: Wrong! It's natural for the body to use lots of energy by moving around and staying active. Exercise is not a waste of time or energy. It keeps the body healthy.

Special exercise

Some people need to exercise only certain muscles, for example, if they have an injury or disability. For example, a cycling machine makes the legs work well while protecting a back injury. Swimming helps to keep muscles busy while supporting a painful joint.

Practical advice

Warm up, cool down

Athletes and sports people do gentle warm-up exercises such as bending, stretching, and jogging before they start training or playing. These exercises gradually get harder. This helps prepare the body for the main action. Afterwards, cool-down exercises prevent muscles and joints from becoming stiff.

Which sports are best?

Most sports are good for the muscles and the body. But not all sports suit everyone. Each person should try several sports or games, to find the best one to keep fit and have fun. If you find a sport or exercise too difficult, you are probably less likely to carry on with it.

🔍 **Swimming is a good all-round form of exercise that involves most muscles in the body.**

Everyone is different

Organized sports are a great way to exercise muscles and stay healthy. Because everyone is different in body size, shape, and abilities, certain people are suited to particular sports. For example, a short person might not be good at basketball but could be good at long-distance running. A person who is not so skilled at ball sports might be a great swimmer. It's a matter of finding the best sport for you.

Having fun

Sports and games are also helpful because they can be satisfying and fun. People try to do better each time they play. In team sports, you can make friends and enjoy helping the whole team to win.

 We are the champions! It feels great to take part in a sport.

 SCIENCE BEHIND THE MYTH

MYTH: It's best to have lots of bulging muscles.

SCIENCE: Not always. It depends on the sport or exercise. Long-distance runners do not usually have lots of bulging muscles. In fact, many of them are quite slim and light.

17

What are muscle skills?

It takes more than just strong muscles to be good at sport and exercise. Muscle skills are also important.

Practice

Most activities and sports need good reactions, timing, balance, and co-ordination to help muscles work together to make movements smooth and accurate. For example, to catch a ball you move your hands to the correct place, watch the ball all the way into your hands, and grasp the ball at the right time. This is known as hand–eye co-ordination.

Practical advice

Practising muscle skills

Throw a tennis ball against a wall from about 3 metres (10 feet) away. Try to hit the same spot on the wall every time, and catch the ball as it comes back. After 20 throws, take a step back and repeat the exercise. As you keep practising, your hand–eye co-ordination will improve.

Coaching and equipment

People do better at sports and games if they learn properly. This usually means having a trainer or coach to give advice, to show you the correct way to do things, and to help you avoid problems such as strained muscles or sprained joints.

Correct kit and equipment are also vital, not only for better performance, but for safety. For example, in organized cycle racing, everyone has to wear a helmet. The right kind of equipment, along with coaching, plenty of practice, and avoiding risks, all make sport much safer.

🔍 **A skier's brilliant balance develops over years of practice.**

Do muscles get "hungry"?

Your muscles need fuel to power their movements. The fuel comes from the food you eat. This food energy is brought to muscles through the blood. It is pumped by another muscle, the heart, which also needs a fuel supply.

🔍 **This sprinter's muscles are working hard to help him run fast.**

Blood sugar

The main food substance that muscles use for energy is **glucose**. It comes from the breakdown of substances called **carbohydrates** in food. When in the blood, glucose is usually called blood glucose or blood sugar.

Muscles need another substance to break apart blood sugar and get energy – oxygen. It comes from the air you breathe into your lungs. The oxygen goes from the lungs into the blood, which takes it to your muscles.

Aerobic exercise

As muscles work harder, they need more blood sugar and more oxygen. So the lungs and heart work faster in order to supply the extra blood carrying oxygen and glucose. This type of activity, using lots of oxygen that the body gets by breathing harder and faster, is called **aerobic** exercise.

SCIENCE BEHIND THE MYTH

MYTH: Snacks are bad for you.

SCIENCE: Not always! Fruit and specially made sports bars usually have energy that the body can use quickly. Other foods, such as meat, do not provide energy quickly. Very sugary snacks such as chocolate are not so good since the body cannot cope with lots of sugar in a very short time.

Which is the most important muscle?

One muscle in your body never stops working. Your whole body depends on it. This muscle is your heart.

A bag of muscle

The heart is like a bag of muscle. It pumps or beats at least once every second. During each beat the heart first fills with blood. Then it **contracts** powerfully to squeeze out the blood, along the **blood vessels** to all body parts.

Extreme body fact

The heart's beating speed can be measured by the **pulse rate** in the wrist. This varies depending on a person's age, fitness, whether they are female or male, and what they are doing.

- Young babies have a rate of 110–120 beats per minute.
- This slows to about 60–80 for an adult at rest.
- Jogging puts the pulse rate up to 90–100.
- Very hard exercise increases pulse rate to more than 150.

Faster and harder

Like other muscles, the heart needs plenty of regular activity to stay strong and healthy. This is why sports and exercise are good for the body.

SCIENCE BEHIND THE MYTH

MYTH: Eating too much before exercise is bad.

SCIENCE: This is true. After a big meal, lots of blood flows to the stomach and guts, to collect the digested food. This leaves less blood for the muscles and brain.

The way the heart beats during excercise can be watched on a screen to make sure all is well.

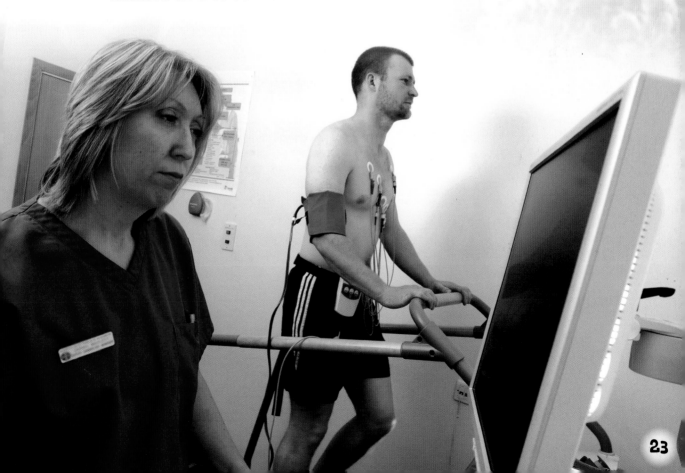

Which problems affect muscles?

Muscles can suffer injuries and other problems, just as other body parts can. But usually muscles heal well with no lasting effects.

Pulls, strains, and tears

A pulled or strained muscle happens when the muscle tries to work too hard and some of its tiny **muscle fibres** are damaged. It may also happen if the muscle is stretched suddenly, such as in a fall or accident. It usually mends in a few days. A torn muscle is when many tiny fibres break. This is more serious than a pull or strain. A bad muscle tear may need an operation to join the torn parts with stitches or clips.

SCIENCE BEHIND THE MYTH

MYTH: People shiver when they are scared.

SCIENCE: Some people think we shiver when we are afraid. But usually it's when we are cold. Shivering is what happens when muscles twitch. As they twitch, they give off heat that warms the body.

Painful cramp

Muscle cramp is when a muscle tries to **contract** on its own, without you wanting it to. The muscle becomes hard and painful. Cramp may happen when you suddenly use a muscle a great deal, after not using it much. The muscle quickly becomes very tired. Another reason is when the body loses lots of water, for example as sweat, and the water is not replaced by drinking. This is known as dehydration.

Practical advice

How to ease cramp

Try to stretch the body part so the muscle is pulled longer – a friend can help to do this. Rub or massage the muscle.

How do I look after my muscles?

Busy muscles are healthy muscles. If you keep on the move, stay active, and take regular exercise, your muscles will be fit and strong.

Making faces

Apart from the big muscles in your legs and arms, there are hundreds of smaller muscles all over the body. More than 50 are in your face, including muscles in your lips, cheeks, eyelids, and forehead. They need to keep active, too. You use them to eat, drink, wink, blink, talk, raise your eyebrows, smile, and frown. To see them at work, look in a mirror and make some funny faces!

Extreme body fact

Pardon?
The body's smallest muscle is the stapedius, not much bigger than this letter "l". It's deep inside your ear. Its job is to pull on the tiny ear bones when sounds are too loud. This prevents too much **vibration** of the ear bones, which might otherwise cause ear damage or even deafness.

A quick wink is one of the few actions that uses just one muscle.

SCIENCE BEHIND THE MYTH

MYTH: It takes fewer muscles to smile than it does to frown.

SCIENCE: Scientists disagree about whether people use more muscles to smile or to frown, and it takes different amounts of effort to make a small smile, a broad grin, or a big frown. However, if you smile and are happy, you are more likely to be active, instead of sitting around doing little with your other muscles.

Your amazing muscles

Your bendiest muscle is your tongue. Some people can curl their tongue into a U shape or even into an upside-down U!

The eyelid muscles blink around 10,000 times each day.

The muscles in the forearm that bend the fingers are called digital flexors.

Your longest muscles are the left and right sartorius. Each one stretches from your hip down your thigh to your knee.

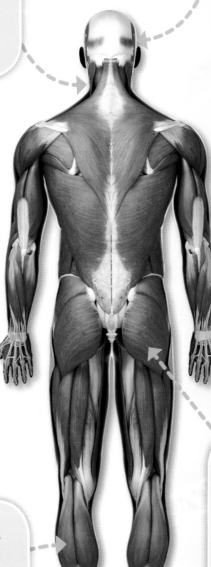

Your strongest muscles for their size are the temporalis and masseter on each side of your head. They work your jaws so you can eat.

To nod and shake your head you use muscles in your neck.

The forearm muscles that straighten the fingers are called digital extensors.

You sit on your biggest muscles. They are the two gluteus maximus muscles, left and right, which are in your bottom.

You stand on tip-toe by **contracting** your calf muscles.

Glossary

aerobic process that needs oxygen, such as aerobic exercise

blood vessel tube through which blood travels around the body

carbohydrates in food, substances containing carbon, hydrogen, and oxygen, which includes sugars and also starches in foods such as rice, potatoes, and pasta

cardiac muscle special kind of muscle that makes up the walls of the heart, and which never gets tired or fatigued

contract to get smaller or become shorter

filaments long, thin strands, such as the protein filaments inside myofibrils

glucose sugar, the main energy-providing fuel for muscles

muscle fibre thin, string-like part that forms bundles inside muscles

myofibril extremely thin, long strand that forms bundles inside muscle fibres

protein substance that forms many parts and structures inside the body, including skin and muscles

pulse rate number of pulsations or bulges per minute in the body's blood vessels, usually felt in the wrist, which shows the heart's beating rate

skeletal muscle muscle that pulls on the bones of the skeleton; also known as striated or voluntary muscle

smooth muscle muscle with no pattern of striations or bands seen under the microscope; also known as involuntary muscle

tendon strong, rope-like part that joins a muscle to a bone

vibration when something shakes very fast, usually many times each second

Find out more

Books

Mighty Muscular-Skeletal System: How Do My Bones and Muscles Work?, John Burstein (Crabtree, 2009)

Move Your Body: Bones and Muscles (Freestyle Express: Body Talk), Steve Parker (Raintree, 2006)

The Skeleton and Muscles (The Human Machine), Louise Spilsbury (Heinemann Library, 2009)

Websites

www.cyh.com/HealthTopics/HealthTopicDetailsKids. aspx?p=335&np=152&id=2457

Visit this website to find loads of information about muscles and how to keep them healthy.

kidshealth.org/kid/stay_healthy/fit/work_it_out.html

Find out why exercise is cool!

yucky.discovery.com/flash/body/pg000123.html

The yucky people give the lowdown on muscles on this website.

Index